RESTORATION FOR YOUR HISTORIC DOOR

Written by: Mitchell Kilby

www.lowbudgetwindowrestoration.com

While the author has made every effort to provide accurate internet addresses and links at the time of publication, the author does not assume any responsibility for errors or changes that occur after publication.

Further, the author has no control over and assumes no responsibility for the author or third-party websites or their content.

GENERAL DISCLAIMER:

THE AUTHOR ASSUMES NO LIABILITY FOR PROPERTY DAMAGE, BODILY INJURY, OR DEATH INCURRED AS A RESULT OF ANY OF THE INFORMATION CONTAINED IN THE CONTENT OF THE BOOK GENERALLY. USE THIS INFORMATION AT YOUR OWN RISK. THE AUTHOR RECOMMENDS SAFE PRACTICES WHEN WORKING WITH TOOLS SEEN OR IMPLIED IN THE PICTURES, WRITTEN CONTENT, AND ANY METHODS CONTAINED IN THE INSTRUCTIONS.

FURTHER, THE AUTHOR RECOMMENDS SAFE PRACTICES IF WORKING WITH ANY LEAD PAINT, ASBESTOS-CONTAINING MATERIALS, TOOLS, MATERIALS GENERALLY, EQUIPMENT, OR WITH GLASS.

DUE TO FACTORS BEYOND THE AUTHOR'S CONTROL, NO INFORMATION CONTAINED IN THIS BOOK OR ON ANY ASSOCIATED WEBPAGES OR APPS (SUCH AS AN INSTAGRAM OR FACEBOOK ACCOUNT), INCLUDING ASSOCIATED THIRD-PARTY WEBPAGES OR APPS, SHALL CREATE ANY EXPRESSED OR IMPLIED WARRANTY OR GUARANTEE OF ANY PARTICULAR RESULT.

ANY INJURY, DAMAGE, DEATH, OR LOSS THAT MAY RESULT FROM THE USE OF THE INFORMATION CONTAINED IN THIS BOOK IS THE SOLE RESPONSIBILITY OF THE YOU, THE READER, AND NOT THE AUTHOR. USE THE INFORMATION FROM THIS BOOK AND ANY THIRD-PARTY WEBSITES AT YOUR OWN RISK.

Illustrations by: Sam Perez (Instagram @bikemuffin)

Dedicated to CW Raetzsch, who helped guide the way.

HOW TO USE THIS BOOK

"Don't Panic" ~ Douglas Adams

READ THROUGH IT ONCE BEFORE STARTING

I recommend reading through all the steps in this book at least once before starting. Just like reading a recipe once before cooking a new dish, it will be helpful to read through this book before starting so you'll have a general understanding of the entire process.

WRITTEN FOR DO-IT-YOURSELFERS

I made this book for do-it-yourselfers with limited to no knowledge of carpentry, painting, staining, varnishing, etc.

I made this book for people like myself who bought an old house with no idea what I was doing and had to learn along the way.

WRITTEN FOR HISTORIC DOORS

While some of the principles in this book apply to newer doors, this book is designed for historic doors. I consider a "historic door" to be one that is at least 50 years old and made of solid wood. They may or may not have a glass window in them. This book includes sections on working with glass if you have a window in your door.

This book is written from an American perspective with the expectation that the audience will primarily be based in North America. However, most principles should also cover historic doors in other locations. But if your door is hundreds of years old, like one might be in Europe, you may want to consult with a local craftsperson to get their advice.

I LOVE HEARING YOUR STORIES

If you use this book to restore a door, whether here in the US or elsewhere, and you find it helpful, please contact me and tell me your story! I would love to hear it.

I can be reached at www.lowbudgetwindowrestoration.com. That is my website, where I primarily focus on restoring historic wood and metal windows. Please visit the site and join a course! I have over 8 hours of tutorial videos on the website designed to help do-it-yourselfers restore their historic windows.

TABLE OF CONTENTS

INTRODUCTION

Welcome!

This book will show you step-by-step how I restored my historic door. I made this guide to help people save their historic doors and give them some thoughts and encouragement.

When I first thought about restoring my 100-year-old door, I felt overwhelmed and thought I'd have to get a professional contractor. Luckily, my neighbor owned a local store called "The Old Door Store," and he gave me the instruction and reassurance I needed to tackle it myself.

In this book, I use text and pictures to explain my process. My door needed everything except professional carpentry, so this guide should hopefully cover most of the steps required to restore your door.

In total, there are 31 steps in this guide. Don't let that scare you. Many steps take just a few minutes to complete. Just take it step-by-step, and you'll get there.

*Note: This guide may not work if your door is severely rotted. You may need to get professional carpentry help. But at least you can restore the rest of the door by following this guide, saving you some money.

Note: This guide follows the steps for a front door. But you can also use these same techniques to restore your interior doors. Just cut out the steps you don't need.

I restored an interior door to my house following many steps in this book. For interior doors, just skip the steps that don't apply.

A picture of my awesome neighbor CW, who ran the "Old Door Store" for many years. Here he brought his granddaughter to inspect my progress on the door. He taught me many of the steps in this book.

BEFORE AND AFTER

Before:

When we first bought the house, we loved the door. My neighbor called it a "cathedral door" because it had a pointed window. It was a beautiful door, but the sun had faded and dried it out severely. It had pieces missing, as I'll show below. Overall, it was a basket case.

After:

Here is the door after restoration. It now looks beautiful, and the wood has been hydrated and restored. The holes have been patched, and the hardware is working fabulously. The glass is securely in place and has new glaze. It is now one of the showpieces of the house.

RECOMMENDED TOOLS AND MATERIALS

In this book, I mention the tools and materials below throughout the various steps. Here is the comprehensive list. You may already have many of these tools, and they may not all be necessary for you. But they are the tools I used and suggest using in the various steps.

Electric Tools:

- Random Orbit Sander	https://a.co/d/cxhnrT5
- 80-grit pads	https://a.co/d/g8Jswc8
- 220 grit-pads	https://a.co/d/5WAZVXE
- Cordless Drill	https://a.co/d/6RmGDXr
- Dremel Tool	https://a.co/d/2tBfxzU
- Cheaper version	https://a.co/d/2tBfxzU

Handheld Tools:

- Hammer	https://a.co/d/6RmGDXr
- Flat head screwdriver (normal sized)	https://a.co/d/0RAo9c9
- Flat head screwdriver (small-sized for old screws)	https://a.co/d/h9zzJSi
- Philips head screwdriver	https://a.co/d/ezNeL0T
- Stainless Steel Pry Bar Scraper	https://a.co/d/411lkPH
- Purdy Painter's multitool	https://a.co/d/bc0rS6x
- Nail punch	https://a.co/d/6tuSRgR
- Hand Planer (*optional*)	https://a.co/d/cebE8zg
- Nail Nipper	https://a.co/d/c5H6kgk

Paint Removing Materials and Tools:

(See Step 8 for more explanation on paint removal)

Chemical Strippers (if you plan to strip the old paint chemically):

- Citristrip Stripping Gel https://a.co/d/5RD6jbf
- (or) Smartstrip Paint Remover https://a.co/d/hmu3XpI
- Laminated Strips (helpful, but not necessary) https://a.co/d/4Uaio0w
- Plastic Knives https://a.co/d/6rcCDlB
- Wire brush https://a.co/d/6Nrfl1Z
- Vinegar (get at a grocery store)

Scrapers (if you plan to scrape off the old paint) - Choose between a Hand Scraper or a Vacuum Scraper

- Hand Scraper *https://a.co/d/axw3A60*

OR:

- Vacuum scraper (the "Proscraper") *https://bit.ly/3D8Blnc*
- HEPA Shop Vac *https://a.co/d/6KcTXdm*

Infrared Strippers (if you plan to use heat to strip old paint)

- EcoStrip Speed Heater *https://bit.ly/3DeEP7M*

General Materials:

- Plywood (to board up your door frame)(get at the hardware store)
- Torx Screws (to board up your door frame) https://a.co/d/3GbkekV
- Liquid Wood (or Minwax Wood Putty below) https://a.co/d/6DFguxY
- Minwax Wood Putty https://a.co/d/6DFguxY
- Microfiber towels https://a.co/d/dGYrsbS
- Cheesecloth https://a.co/d/8PxGQIr

If Your Door has a Window, Get This Too:

- Glaze - Sarco, Dual Glaze Version https://bit.ly/3xeUcsV
- Whiting *https://bit.ly/3Ryp1Rw*
- Finish Nails
    - 1 inch: https://a.co/d/dxPOs8c
    - ¾ inch: https://a.co/d/ioJMGz9

Paint Brushes:

- Foam Brush https://a.co/d/4NkekG4
- Flat Brush https://a.co/d/1mPvLHl
- Cheap Brushes (for priming) https://a.co/d/dM5yma8
- Finish Brush:
    - Wooster Brush: https://a.co/d/4Nw8ttC
    - Alternatively, a Purdy Brush: https://a.co/d/2MENOtZ
- Paint Brush Cover https://a.co/d/eNTeaY6

Paints ***(all recommendations are water-based paint):***

- Primer - PPG's Seal Grip Gripper Primer https://thd.co/3L9U6bW

- Interior Paint, Sherman Williams's Trim https://bit.ly/3U12oqk

- Exterior Paint - specialized for front doors https://a.co/d/hGXUWqg

- Frosted Glass Spray (*optional*) https://a.co/d/dfwX3Lo

Stain and Varnishes:

- Stains - I like Minwax stains and the gunstock color. Obtain at Hardware Store.

- Varnish Finish

    - An oil-based Polyurethane https://a.co/d/day228n
    - Alternatively, a spar varnish https://a.co/d/94yLy0E

Protective Equipment:

- N100 Mask https://a.co/d/93jH10f
- Painters Plastic Drop Cloth https://a.co/d/102aJQg

*Note: If you want to experiment and go all out with your restoration, look up a company called Earth and Flax. They sell linseed oil paints that closely match many early paints, making them the most historically accurate. https://www.earthandflax.com

STEP ONE

ASSESS YOUR DOOR

TOOLS/MATERIALS NEEDED: *None*

The first step is to assess your door. Determine its condition. Even though it may be in rough shape, you can likely save it!

My door was in horrible shape. It was dried out. Discolored. It had missing chunks and mismatched hardware. The wood on the outside needed to be restored, the paint on the inside was cracked, and the door needed repainting.

For Rotted Doors: This book does not cover repairing rotted doors. If your door is rotted, several online videos demonstrate how to replace the bottom of your door if the rot is extensive.

A video showing the process using carpentry and carpentry tools:

https://www.youtube.com/watch?v=w4RW2DHIEGQ

Another video using wood filler – probably a more accessible process:

https://www.youtube.com/watch?v=AuGdp-AgGgg

Rotted Door Jam: Additionally, you may have a rotted door jam/frame. If this is the case, you likely should reach out to a professional craftsperson to help problem solve. If you want to try it yourself, here is a video showing some instructions:

https://www.youtube.com/watch?v=AuGdp-AgGgg

Hopefully, these rot problems don't exist for you.

Overall, no matter how rough your door is, you can save it unless it is almost entirely rotted away.

STEP TWO
GET PLYWOOD TO BOARD UP YOUR DOOR AREA

TOOLS/MATERIALS NEEDED: *Plywood, Cordless Drill, Torx Screws, Torx Drill Bit*

Unless you can finish your door in one day, you'll need to board up the space where your front door goes.

Here is what worked best for me:

- Use Strong, thick Plywood. If you are in an area with potentially higher crime rates, use stronger plywood and screw the plywood into the siding or trim around the door.

- Use Star Patterned Screws ("Torx Screws"). And don't forget a Torx bit for your drill. The advantage of a Torx screw is that a person with a drill or screwdriver can't just walk up and unscrew the plywood around the door frame. They would at least need a Torx bit. Anything you can do to slow down thieves is always helpful, and making them get a particular bit is a good start.

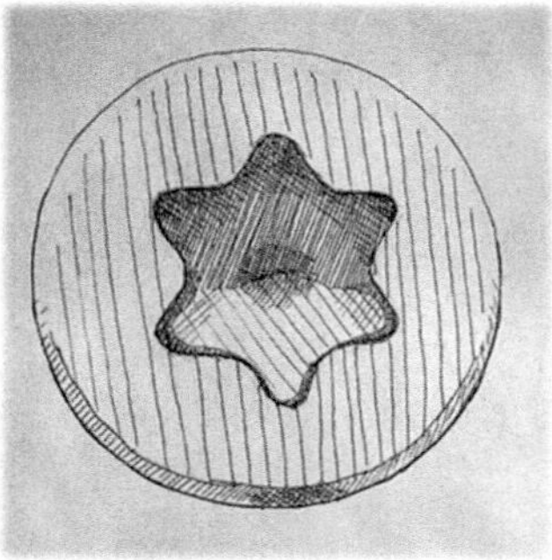

- Make it Wide Enough. Measure the plywood to be wide enough to go beyond the width of the door frame by about six inches on each side so that you can screw the boards into the siding/frame.

- Additional Piece on the Inside. If you're more concerned about security, or if you will be away from your house in the evenings or for an extended period, you can also choose to install an additional piece of plywood on the inside of the door frame as an extra barrier to any thieves. That way, even if they get through the first outside layer, they still must go through the second inside layer.

- Installing on the Outside. To me, it's nice just to screw it into the outside, as it's often easier to paint and hide the screw holes.

How you choose to board your door frame is ultimately up to you! I suggest making sure that you have one or two pieces of plywood ready to go before you start your project so that you can board up the door area after you've pulled the door off without having to take a trip to the hardware store in between.

A picture of my house boarded up during restoration.

STEP THREE
REMOVE THE DOOR FROM THE FRAME

TOOLS/MATERIALS NEEDED: *Normal-sized Flathead Screwdriver, Hammer*

To remove the door, lift the pins holding the hinges in place. I don't have a video for this, but here is one from online. The first few minutes discuss this process.

https://www.youtube.com/watch?v=AuGdp-AgGgg

STEP FOUR
REMOVE ALL HARDWARE

TOOLS/MATERIALS NEEDED: *Normal-sized Flathead Screwdriver, Small-sized Flathead Screwdriver, Phillips head screwdriver*

Next, remove any hardware on the door: Hinges, Locks, Latches, Handles, Etc.

There was not as much standardization in the past, so each door will have slightly different hardware. But all of it is self-explanatory in that you simply begin to unscrew the screws and find what is hidden behind the paint. Often, you'll need to unscrew an outside plate, and then you'll be able to slide out the lock, etc.

*Make sure to keep all screws and pieces. Put everything in a plastic Ziploc bag. Most parts are not replaceable. It can also be helpful to take pictures along the way to help you remember what it looked like before you took it apart.

Learn to Make Your Hardware Dazzle:

Take my free hardware restoration mini-course to learn how to restore hardware to its original beauty! It goes over all the fundamentals of how to restore hardware. It's a fun process!

You can find the "Hardware Restoration" course on my website at:

www.lowbudgetwindowrestoration.com

Getting the Lock Rebuilt by a Locksmith:

As to the lock itself, I suggest taking it to a professional locksmith who knows how to rebuild historic locks. In my city, which has about 2.5M people, I know only one or two locksmiths who can do this. But the one I used was excellent, and she did a fantastic job. She even shined up the old brass on the outside *and* the inside.

As soon as you pull the lock, go ahead, and take it to the locksmith so they can hopefully finish before you reinstall your door.

Before:

After:

Investigating the History of Old Hardware

I always think it's fun to research details about the hardware I find in historic houses. They are an example of America's manufacturing history, and you can find great historical information on the internet.

After my locksmith cleaned up my lock, I could see the name of the lock manufacturer, Clinton Lock Company.

After some sleuthing on the internet, I found that Clinton Lock Company was once established in Clinton, Iowa. I've ridden my bike across Iowa several times and have been near Clinton, so I found this interesting.

Here are some pictures gathered by the Burke Museum, an online genealogical museum for the Burke Family of Clinton, Iowa. I don't know who owns the copyright to this picture, but I will attribute it to the Burke Museum and Nellie Hughes, who donated the photo to them.

It is cool to know my lock was made right in this building, possibly by the people listed below.

The Clinton Lock Company manufactured locks, reportedly of all sizes. David and Frank Ogden inherited the company from an uncle and managed the piecework assembly of products which ranged "from the most inexpensive rim locks to the highest type of special construction for use on any type of building from the cottage to the skyscraper. Daily production is sufficient to equip 1,000 ordinary homes with locks, window trim and all necessary builders' hardware."
Courtesy of The Clinton Herald

The boxing department (opposite) at one time had the following employees on one shift: Legouri McConohy, Harold Boysen, Nellie Clark Hughes, Tommye Sheean, Edna Goettsch, Agnes Judge and Maxine Meeder Hayes.
In the packing department, (below), employees worked on three assembly lines. The front row (left to right) was Annaora Hacker, Legouri McConohy; second row: Unidentified, Edna Goettsch, Nellie Clark Hughes, Agnes Judge Glendenning and on the third line Eleanor Reinke.
Photos Courtesy of Nellie M. Hughes

STEP FIVE

SPREAD OUT A SOFT TOWEL NEARBY

TOOLS/MATERIALS NEEDED: *A towel or moving blanket*

<u>*If your door has no window, skip this step.</u>

If you have a window in the door, the next step after this will be to remove the glass. But once you remove the glass, you'll need a soft but firm place ready to put it.

You'll want to have that ready before you pull the glass so that you're not standing there holding the glass and looking around for a place to put it.

Grab a towel or blanket now to lay the glass somewhere after removing it.

Here is a picture of my glass resting on a towel after I removed it.

STEP SIX
REMOVE MOLDING STRIPS AROUND THE GLASS

TOOLS/MATERIALS NEEDED: *Stainless Steel Pry Bar Scraper, Painter's Multitool*

*If your door has no window, skip this step.

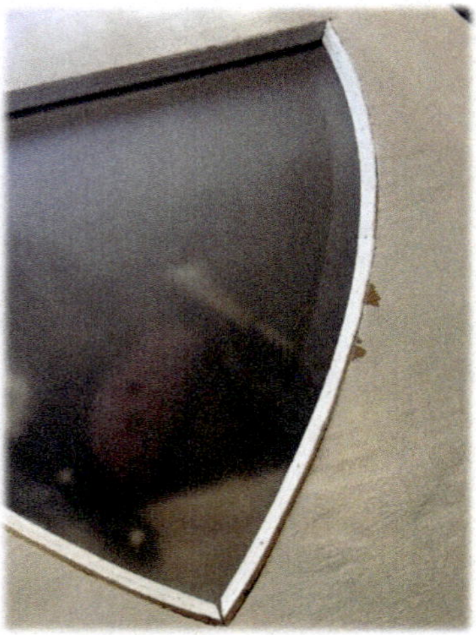

If you have original glass on your door, it's very special. You don't want to break it.

You can likely avoid removing the glass if you're just repainting the door. But if you're doing a complete restoration, I suggest removing the glass to ensure that it doesn't get broken and so you can adequately reinstall it later using a new glaze.

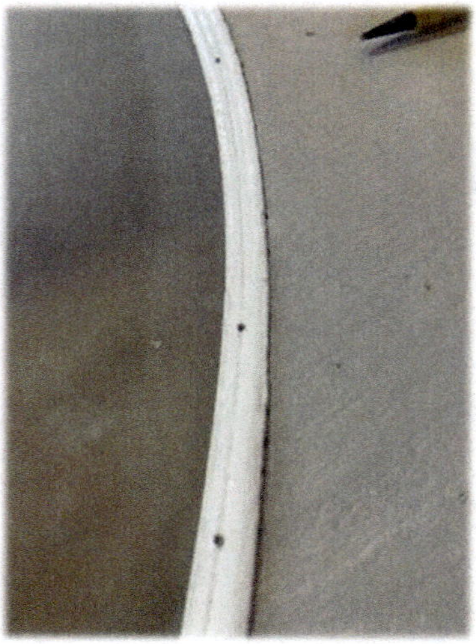

Likely, your glass is held by small little wooden molding strips. These strips are called "molding." The molding will have tiny finishing nails in them. Gently pull the strips off using the Stainless Steel Prybar, a Painter's Multitool, or a thin flat screwdriver. The wood strips should eventually begin to pull away, and you can use nail nippers (basically nail plyers) to remove the nails (as described below).

*Note: The Stainless-Steel Pry Bar Scraper (found here: https://a.co/d/411lkPH) is an essential and excellent tool, and I strongly suggest getting one.

Once the molding strips are out, be very careful with them. On a square window, you might be able to replace the molding strips. But on my door, they were curved and irreplaceable. If I had broken one, I'd have had to call in a custom fabricator, which could have been expensive.

Now grab a nail nipper. Nail nippers are excellent for holding onto nails and pulling them through the wood.

Use the nail nipper to pull the nails out of the molding. Pull them from the backside, not from the top. In other words, pull them through from the bottom of the nail sticking out from the molding, not from the top of the nail. Doing this will help preserve your wood. (This assumes the nails have no head, which they shouldn't if they are finishing nails. Pull them from the top as carefully as possible if they have a nail head for some weird and wild reason.)

Now, if the nails pull through the molding when you dislodge it and are stuck in the main part of the door, go ahead and use the nail nippers to pull the nails out of the door. You can pull from the nail head in this situation.

Here is an example of another historic door with glass. The door is from a river cabin that my great-grandparents built. You can easily see the molding strips on this door.

In this picture on the right, the bottom molding piece is removed so you can more easily see the difference.

STEP SEVEN

PULL THE GLASS OUT & CLEAN UP

TOOLS/MATERIALS NEEDED: *Stainless Steel Pry Bar Scraper, Painter's Multitool*

<u>*If your door has no window, skip this step.</u>

Once the molding strips are removed, remove the glass by pushing/pulling the glass out with slight pressure from your hands. If it is not popping out easily, you may need to use a razor blade to gently cut any remaining glaze on the back side of the glass opposite the strips you just removed. If someone has replaced the glass within the last 20 years, you may have to cut silicone which can be tedious. You may need some help to hold the door steady during this process.

After you pull the glass out, lay it on a towel or blanket on a table and keep it safe and out of the way for now.

Next, scrape out any remaining glaze, silicone, or debris left in the channels where the glass was sitting. You will need this channel clean when you put the glass back in later.

By the way, this channel is called a "rabbit."

Missing or Broken Glass:

If your door is missing its glass or the glass is broken, you can call a glass shop, and they can fabricate the new glass for you. If you'd like to try and obtain original wavy glass, reach out to an architectural restoration shop in your city and see if they can pull some glass for you that you can take to a glass shop to cut to shape.

STEP EIGHT
REMOVE OLD PAINT

TOOLS/MATERIALS NEEDED: *Depends on the removal option you choose (see below)*

One or both sides of your door are likely covered in several layers of paint. You can choose to remove the paint yourself, or you can see if you can send the door out to a professional "door dipper."

Protect yourself:

A primary issue here is that you may have lead-based paint. Many historic doors do, so make sure you take proper precautions.

If you decide to strip the door yourself, wear a proper mask (I recommend an N-100 mask) and other appropriate PPE.

Remove the door and working area away from your living spaces and keep children and animals away. I suggest also laying a plastic drop cloth down under the space where you're working so that you can wrap it up later and throw it away to prevent any dust captured from ending up on your floor. Do your research and use your head.

My preferred method - Scraping:

If you're going to remove the paint yourself, my favorite method is to simply scrape the paint off. This worked very well for me. I used a "proscraper" tool hooked to a HEPA shop vac, and it just sucked all the dust and paint chips right into the vacuum. The proscrapers are very sharp and just took the paint right off for me. I also liked the proscrapers because there is no sticky residue left over, as there can be with a chemical stripper. However, I'm also a big guy who can put a lot of force into the scraper. If this is not an option, a chemical stripper or infrared heat stripper might work better for you. This picture to the right is my door after I scraped it clean. Remember, you don't have to get ALL the old paint off, just most of it, especially the loose paint.

Others like using inferred heaters. This is a good blog entry from some house rehabbers who swore off chemical stripping and decided they liked using the Speedheater tool best: https://rehabdorks.com/2017/04/dont-strip-paint-before-reading-this/

Different Paint Removal Methods:

- Professional Door Dipping. Some architectural restoration shops still have vats of soda that you can dip a door or window into, and it will pull off all the old paint. Ask around your city and see if you can find one. It is not often that expensive, which can be a great solution if you have many doors! This will not work for all doors, so talk to the restoration shop. Many architectural restoration shops offer this.

- <u>Chemical Stripper</u>. This method is cheap, and it works. You brush on the stripper (and you can then add plastic strips to the top of it to quicken the process) and let it sit. Come back in the morning or several hours later when you see a lot of paint bubbling up. If you don't see anything, you probably didn't add enough stripper, so just add some more. I like these two versions because they are more natural:

- Citristrip Stripping Gel	https://a.co/d/5RD6jbf
- (or) Smartstrip Paint Remover	https://a.co/d/hmu3XpI
- Laminated Strips (helpful, not necessary)	https://a.co/d/4Uaio0w
- Plastic Knives	https://a.co/d/6rcCDlB
- Wire brush	https://a.co/d/6Nrfl1Z
- Vinegar	(get at a grocery store)

When you return, the paint should be softened and off the wood. Then use a plastic knife or painter's multitool to scoop off the old paint. I like a plastic knife because the wood can be more sensitive because of the chemicals, and you don't want to scratch it. You can then use a stiff wire brush and water to remove the remaining residue. If there are still multiple layers left, repeat the process until you see wood again. You can remove stubborn areas of paint with steel wool. I don't recommend sanding yet.

- Finally, neutralize the door with some vinegar diluted in water to about a 1 to 5 ratio. This step will ensure that when you later paint your door, nothing is left under the paint that later causes it to bubble.

- Heat Gun/Inferred Heater. If you're going to restore several doors (like a whole house) or a door and many windows, an inferred heater can work great. They are expensive, in any case. Generally, a setup is around $500 at the time of writing. Alternatively, a heat gun can work and is effective and much cheaper to buy, but they're not always as easy to work with as an inferred heater. I was never a fan of the heat gun. I've listed a quality inferred heater above in the tools list, but here is another link:

  https://eco-strip.com/product/speedheater-ir-system-standard-kit/#reviews

- Scrape. If the paint is dried out, sometimes scraping is a quick and effective way to remove the paint. Be careful of the dust here, and follow the precautions listed above. The picture I included for this step shows my door after scraping it. Scraping was always my favorite method. To scrape, you can use a handheld scraper like those listed in my tools list.

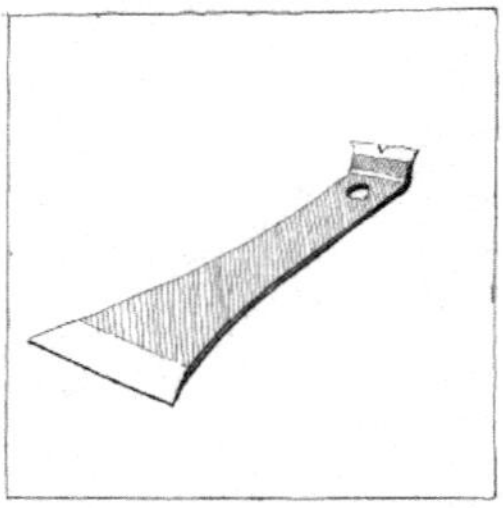

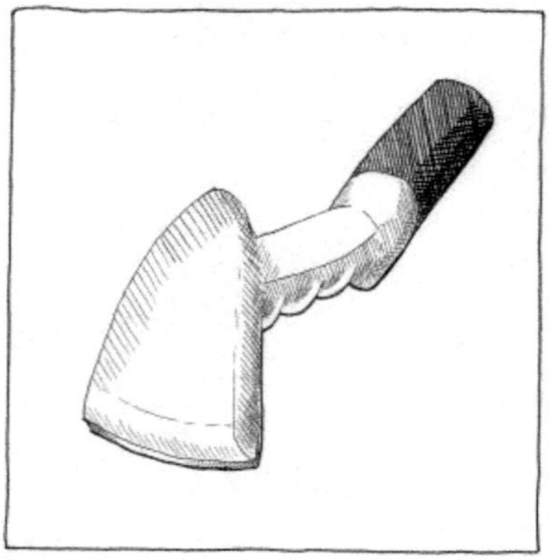

Alternatively, you can get a "proscraper," a magical tool. The proscraper hooks directly to a shop vac, and the combination sucks up any dust. But if lead is a concern (typical on an old door), use a HEPA-rated vacuum.

Find the proscraper in my tools list or here: *https://bit.ly/3D8Blnc*

I used the vacuum in this link to restore my entire house. It's an incredible vacuum. I highly recommend it.

(https://a.co/d/6K08cj0)

*Note: Be careful in delicate areas, such as trim or carved door areas. These pieces may even be molding. They are incredibly fragile if you're scraping. I suggest either not touching the area if the paint is still in good condition or using a chemical stripper and only using a plastic knife to scrape off the old paint in these areas.

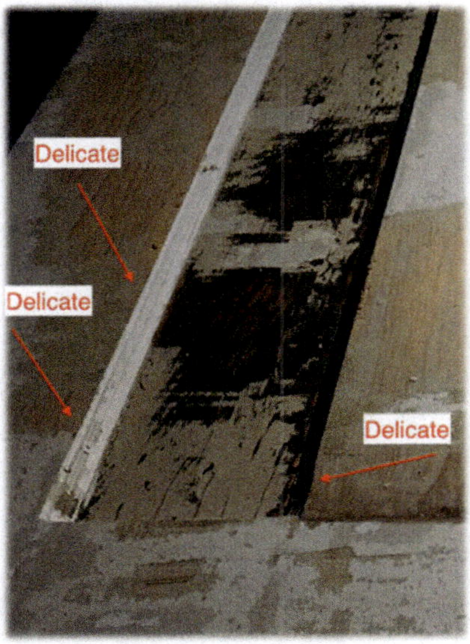

As you can see in the picture on the left, I mostly left the trim alone on my door. That's why the delicate trim strip is still white in the image. When I finished the door, an unfamiliar person would not be able to tell that I had not stripped the paint in these small delicate areas.

If you have an area where you can't use the orbital sander, you can fold the sanding disk and use it for sanding the hard-to-reach area. I couldn't use the orbital sander on my door to sand the thin, sunken areas, so I used this technique.

STEP NINE
REMOVE ANY ROT

TOOLS/MATERIALS NEEDED: *Dremmel Tool, Painter's Multitool*

If your door has rot like mine, the next step is to grind away any rotted areas. Notice the holes in my door here.

This is assuming the rotted areas are small. If they are large areas, such as the entire bottom of your door, then you likely need to replace those areas with new wood and should seek a professional carpenter for help with that.

If it is a smaller area, you can get rid of the rot with a rotary Dremel tool or even a razor blade so that the area is ready to be filled with wood filler.

Here again, is a video from YouTube showing some of that process. The video shows how to remove the rotted areas starting at about Minute 9:00:

https://www.youtube.com/watch?v=AuGdp-AgGgg

STEP TEN
USE WOOD FILLERS TO FILL ROTTED AREAS, HOLES, AND GAPS

TOOLS/MATERIALS NEEDED: *Wood Filler, Painter's Multitool*

Once you've removed any wood rot, it's time to fill the missing areas with a wood filler. There are many types of wood filler. My favorite is "Liquid Wood," an epoxy that – once mixed – becomes a wooden-like substance. Other people like to use Bondo, the same stuff used to patch cars after accidents but designed for wood surfaces. Then there is just good 'ol wood filler, like that made by Minwax.

If you patch a hole on a painted side, you can use any of these fillers with no problem.

If you're going to patch holes on a side you plan to varnish/stain, you need to get a stainable wood filler.

For my door, as you can see, the wood filler was initially white. I later had to add extra stain and take other steps to ensure it wasn't overly bright compared to the wood. I used liquid wood for this patch. I'm not sure if other stainable fillers might have done better.

Eventually, I even had to use charcoal on it to get the tone of the filler dark enough. More on that is below.

Once you've put in the wood filler, smooth it out with the multitool. Once it dries, sand it smooth, as covered in the next step.

STEP ELEVEN
SAND THE PAINTED SIDES

TOOLS/MATERIALS NEEDED: *Mask, Random-Orbit Sander, Sanding Disks (80-grit), maybe a HEPA Shop Vac*

Again, this step is for sanding the painted sides.

After removing as much paint as possible in the stripping/scraping process, you will now sand the door to get it as close back to the wood as possible. Some areas may be more difficult to sand, and you'll need to use hand sandpaper.

For most sanding, use an electric random-orbit sander. I suggest 80-grit sandpaper to start.

Sand the whole door with the 80-grit. Then go over it once more with 220-grit sandpaper.

You don't have to sand off ALL the old paint. Just smooth what is left. The goal should be to have it look about as sanded as my door in the picture above.

If you feel you're at risk of having lead paint, you can also slightly wet the surface (like with a spray mister) to keep dust to a minimum.

If you want to try something helpful, you can hook a vacuum hose up to the back of the sander and use duct tape to connect it to a HEPA shop vac. Then turn on the vacuum, and it will just suck all the dust through to the vacuum. I did this for all my restoration work.

Also, now they just simply sell this setup on Amazon, with no duct tape required: https://a.co/d/2JpvzQH

Don't forget to sand the sides of the door too!

*Note: Make sure you're wearing a mask when sanding! It doesn't even matter if there is lead in the paint or not. There are other chemicals in paint and varnish that you probably don't want to inhale just as a general life practice. Sand away from your living areas in a well-ventilated area.

STEP TWELVE
REMOVE OLD VARNISH ON ANY VARNISHED SIDE

TOOLS/MATERIALS NEEDED: *Mask, Random-Orbit Sander, Sanding Disks (80-grit), maybe a HEPA Shop Vac*

It is likely that the varnish on your varnished side is old and cracked like it was on my door.

My door had varnish in both good and bad condition. The varnish in good condition was under the door knocker, so it never saw any sun or weather. It was like a time capsule that allowed me to see the varnish's original color. Lucky me!

The varnish in the lousy condition is where the sun had beat on it for years and years, and it had completely eroded.

If your old varnish looks like mine did here, then you can just sand it off with course-grit sandpaper (e.g., 80-grit).

If the varnish is still in decent condition, you can use the chemical stripper to remove it (like in the process listed above for removing paint) or try sanding it off.

Alternatively, if your varnish is in good condition, you may not need to remove it. Just use 220-grit sandpaper to lightly sand it. Wipe it down with a microfiber rag and cheesecloth, and then add a light coat of varnish as described in Step Twenty to create a clean finish.

Don't forget to sand the sides of the door, too!

If you have an area where you can't use the orbital sander, you can fold the sanding disk and use it for sanding the hard-to-reach area. I couldn't use the orbital sander on my door to sand the thin, sunken areas, so I used this technique.

A folded sanding disk.

Don't forget to sand the sides too!

*Note: Make sure you're wearing a mask when sanding! It doesn't even matter if there is lead in the paint or not. There are other chemicals in paint and varnish that you probably don't want to inhale just as a general life practice. Sand away from your living areas in a well-ventilated area.

STEP THIRTEEN
WIPE THE DOOR DOWN

TOOLS/MATERIALS NEEDED: *Microfiber Rag, Cheesecloth*

Now use microfiber rags and some cheesecloth to wipe down the door. Your goal here is to pull off as much remaining dust as possible. This is especially important on the varnished side if you have that.

STEP FOURTEEN
CHOOSE PAINT AND STAIN COLORS

TOOLS/MATERIALS NEEDED: *None*

Now you can choose what paint color you want for any painted side and what stain color you want for any varnished side.

Once you choose a stain color, I suggest staining a random piece of wood first so you can look at and compare the coloring. I tried a stain color in this picture but saw it wasn't quite right compared to the original color, so I changed it slightly.

One stain color I like for antique doors is "gun stock," like the stock of an antique rifle. I think the color gives it a classic look. But there are many colors from which to choose.

As to paint colors, if you want to match your current trim color, you can take a piece of your trim to a paint store, and they can color-match it with a laser.

STEP FIFTEEN

FIRST, CHOOSE A SIDE TO WORK

TOOLS/MATERIALS NEEDED: *None*

This isn't really a step but decide which side of the door you will work on first. The inside or the outside? Once you choose, finish working on that side before moving to the second side. When you move to the other side, rest your finished side on some towels or blankets to ensure it doesn't get scratched up.

***Note: Moving forward in this tutorial, I will start with instructions for the painted side of the door and then follow with instructions for the varnished side.**

QUESTION: Should you paint the sides of the door?

ANSWER: Well, it depends. My general rule of thumb:

- *If the outside of the door is painted*: I like to paint the sides of the door the outside color. That way, when you're walking through the door, there is a seamless look between the exterior color and the door once it's opened.

- *If the outside of the door is varnished*: I like to stain the side of the door the color of the outside but not varnish it. Even though the side of the door is not varnished, the stain color will still give it a finished look and will not look obtrusive like an interior paint would here.

- *For the top and bottom of the door*: I do not paint or varnish the top or bottom sides of the door because the door needs to breathe and release moisture.

STEP SIXTEEN
PRIME

TOOLS/MATERIALS NEEDED: *Throwaway Brush, Primer*

If you're going to paint a side of the door, you're now going to prime the wood on the side to be painted. There are different types of primers you can choose.

Oil-Based Primer:

Professionals often prefer oil-based paints, but I think they are harder to work with, and I prefer water-based latex primers and paints.

Additionally, I'm writing this guide post-pandemic, and oil-based primers have been hard to come by since the pandemic. However, if you find one, ensure it is exterior-rated unless the painted side will be entirely indoors.

*Note: a good thing about oil-based primers is that you can use oil-based paints or water-based latex paints over an oil-based primer. They also adhere and cover well.

*Note: if you want to use an oil-based paint later, you will need to use an oil-based primer now.

A blog review suggesting an oil-based painter I like: https://bit.ly/3queJ98

Water-Based Primer:

I like to use water-based primers because I think they are easier to use. My favorite is called Gripper. It works very well at adhering to the wood and covering old paint. I used it on my entire house, and it has continued to adhere very well over the years. There are many suitable water-based latex primers, so you can always get recommendations from your paint store. See also the Materials List above for my recommendations.

Process:

With primer, less is more. I like to brush small amounts on and then use the brush to push the primer into the wood while spreading it. A small amount can go a long way. Brush in the direction of the wood grain.

*Note: If you want to experiment and go all out with your restoration, look up a company called Earth and Flax. They sell linseed oil paints that closely match many early paints, making them the most historically accurate. So, if you're working on a door from the 1800s or even the early 1900s, you might want to check this site out. They helped recently restore George Washington's house, for example. You need to contact them to find the proper procedure for priming, painting, varnishing, etc.

https://www.earthandflax.com

STEP SEVENTEEN
SAND THE PRIMER AND WIPE DOWN

TOOLS/MATERIALS NEEDED: *Random Orbit Sander, 220-grit Pads, Microfiber Rags*

After the primer has dried, sand the primed area with a light sanding. Use 220-grit sandpaper. Just smooth out the primer so it looks like the primer in the picture. You don't want to sand it off. Just sand it down a bit to smooth it. Be light with the sander!

*Note: Make sure the primer is fully dry. For most oil-based primers (which I find harder to sand), you will typically need to at least wait overnight before sanding.

After a light sanding, use a microfiber cloth to wipe off any remaining dust.

Don't forget, you can always fold a sanding disk in half to reach hard-to-reach areas of the door.

The door after a layer of primer and a quick sanding.

STEP EIGHTEEN: PAINT THE DOOR

TOOLS/MATERIALS NEEDED: *Trim Paint (if painting interior), Exterior Door Paint (if painting exterior), a Good Brush*

After sanding the primer and wiping it down, it's time to paint!

First – back to the paint debate – which type to use? Should you use oil-based paint or water-based paint?

Oil-Based Paint:

Painting professionals swear by oil-based paints, especially on surfaces like doors. Oil-based paints are known to leave a smooth finish and are touted as more durable. Professionals, however, are also better at dealing with the solvents you must use, thinning the paint with solvents, etc.

If you have used oil-based paints in the past and know how to work with them, or you have access to someone who can show you the ins and outs of using an oil-based paint, then go for it!

*Note: Make sure you use an oil-based primer if you plan to use an oil-based paint.

Examples of an Oil-Based Front Door Paint:

Exterior: Rustoleum's Front Door Paint: https://a.co/d/9JwtU7G

Interior Trim: Rustoleum's Satin Trim Paint: https://a.co/d/d1kN84B

Interior Trim: Sherman William's Interior Oil-Based Trim Paint: https://bit.ly/3qeF76T

Water-Based Paint:

I prefer using water-based latex paints. I find them much easier to work with, and I like that the brush can be cleaned easily with water. Also, new technology in these paints makes them harden and act like oil-based paint, so you get many of the same benefits without the high VOCs and other negatives.

Interior Paint Recommendation (Water-based Paint):

I like a satin finish for painting the interior side of a door.

I recommend this paint: https://bit.ly/3U12oqk

This is a unique paint for "trim," and the interior side of the door should have the same finish and sheen as the rest of the trim in your house. I love this stuff and was impressed with it from the start. It has some weighted technology, so it slowly sinks and levels itself after you paint, leaving a nice, smooth finish on interior doors and trim. It is also advertised as having a non-yellowing finish, and I find it very durable. The best part is that because of the weighted technology, it goes on without brush marks and dries hard.

Exterior Side Recommendation (Water-based Paint):

For the exterior side, find a water-based paint designed for exterior doors that can withstand sun and scuffing and go on smoothly. Something like this should work: https://a.co/d/hGXUWqg

You can use the same brush for both the interior and exterior.

Brush Recommendation:

I recommend the Purdy XL brush, 2.5 inches wide, angled: https://a.co/d/7FJBRdC

I like this brush because you can use it for just about anything, but it will work for both your exterior and interior latex paints.

How to Apply the Paint:

Put on a thin coat, and paint in the direction of the grain of the wood. Let it dry, then paint a second and even a third coat for a perfect-looking finish.

Here is a diagram that might help. Start with "A" and paint around any delicate edges of the door first. Then move to "B" and paint up and down with the grain of the wood. Then proceed to "C," then "D," and then "E."

If painting the sides, do the sides last.

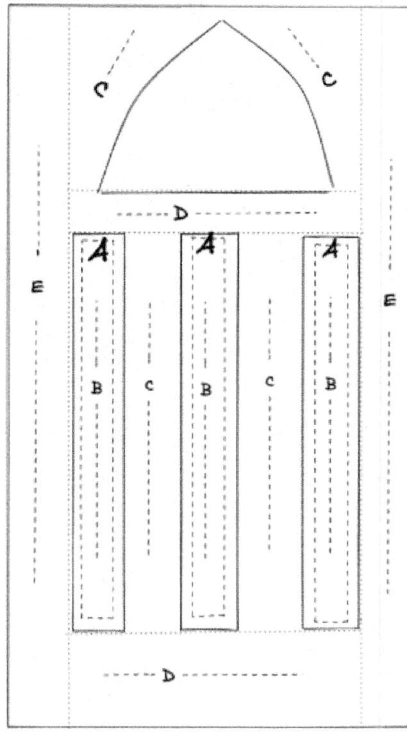

Reminder →General Rule on Painting the Sides of the Door:

If the outside/exterior side of the door is painted: I paint the sides of the door too, but not the top or bottom sides.

If the outside/exterior side is varnished: I like to go ahead and stain the side of the door the color of the outside, but not varnish it.

Either way, don't paint the door's top or bottom. That allows the door to breathe.

*Note: If you want to experiment and go all out with your restoration, look up a company called Earth and Flax. They sell linseed oil paints that closely match many early paints, making them the most historically accurate. So, if you're working on a door from the 1800s or even the early 1900s, you might want to check this site out. They helped recently restore George Washington's house, for example. You need to contact them to find the proper procedure for priming, painting, varnishing, etc.

https://www.earthandflax.com

STEP NINETEEN
STAIN THE DOOR

TOOLS/MATERIALS NEEDED: *Stain, Foam Brush, or Flat Brush*

Ok, now that you've finished the painted side, you can move to the varnished side if you plan to varnish part of the door.

At this point, the side to be varnished should be thoroughly sanded and wiped clean.

If you have filler, you likely can see it, and it is off-colored from the rest of the wood.

It should look something like my door did in this picture. Note the white filler by the lock area.

Apply the Stain.

Before applying the stain, first look at the instructions on the can. Check if your stain type requires any unique application methods.

Start by applying the stain with a foam brush or soft flat brush. Use a small amount first and go from there. Don't overdo it.

Foam Brush: https://a.co/d/4NkekG4

Flat Brush: https://a.co/d/1mPvLHl

Some people also use a rag.

After you apply it, you can wipe off any excess with a clean rag.

Don't forget to sand the sides too!

The door after I've applied some stain.

Add additional coats of stain until you get to the color/darkness you want.

Usually, you will need only two coats of stain.

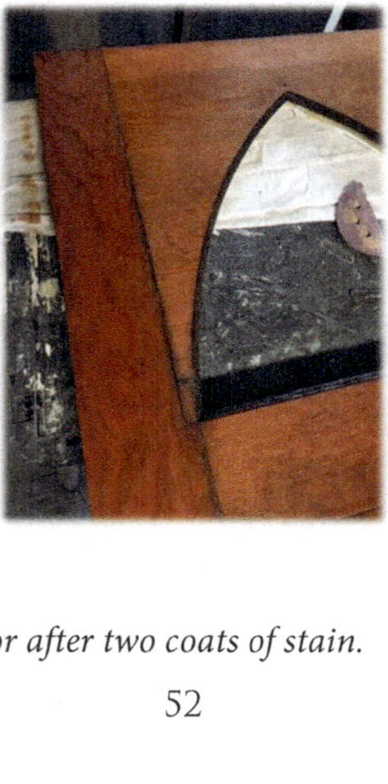

Here are pictures of my door after two coats of stain.

Staining Wood Filler:

If you have wood filler, it may now be off-colored and look a different color than the wood. If you need to darken it, add more stain to the wood filler and let it sink in. To get mine to darken, I also took some charcoal and rubbed it in, which helped darken it.

The left picture is how it looked when I had only stained the wood filler, while the right is after I rubbed it with charcoal. The charcoal gave it a more aged look.

Should you stain the sides of the door?

Rule of thumb - If the door's exterior is going to be varnished and not painted, stain the sides of the door, but do not varnish them.

The sides of the door were stained but not varnished.

STEP TWENTY
APPLY A VARNISH

TOOLS/MATERIALS NEEDED: *Varnish, a good brush as suggested below, Random Orbit Sander, 220-grit sanding pads*

Ok, you are getting close to finishing! Almost there!

You must seal the door with a final coating for this next step. In other words, you need to varnish it.

But what is "Varnish?"

When I say "varnish" in this book, I am using it as a colloquial term for the many types of final coatings you can apply to the varnished side of the door to protect it.

However, there is a difference between final coatings, and there are several varieties, namely: Polyurethane (both oil-based and water-based), Spar Varnish, Shellac, Polycrylic, and Lacquer.

For our purposes here, I recommend using either a Spar Varnish or an oil-based Polyurethane for your final coating.

Spar Varnish: Spar Varnish is an actual finish category and a more traditional door coating. It is often used on boats too. It can be harder to apply because it uses more coats. The "spar" is a part of a boat that endures harsh conditions, so "spar varnish" is a highly durable varnish.

Polyurethane: Polyurethane is a newer form of a final coating that is now used for various wood surfaces.

Here are two articles that go into greater detail:

https://www.hgtv.com/how-to/home-improvement/what-s-the-difference-between-polyurethane--varnish--shellac-and

And

https://www.bobvila.com/articles/varnish-vs-polyurethane/

For my door, I used an oil-based Polyurethane finish. I used an oil-based polyurethane because I was not a professional, and I felt polyurethane would be easier to use. I didn't want to worry about thinning the varnish or other additional steps, and I could use the polyurethane straight out of the box. I otherwise would have used a spar varnish.

The polyurethane that I used has held up well. I restored my door (and took these pictures) five years before writing this tutorial. The door has held up well despite some record-hot summers and full sun on the south-facing door during the summers.

For this tutorial, I will explain from the perspective of applying an oil-based Polyurethane; however, using a spar varnish is similar, so just follow these instructions for the spar varnish as well.

Here is a good article on applying spar varnish: https://repaintnow.com/spar-urethane/

For sheen, I recommend using satin or semi-gloss. I liked how satin looked.

An oil-based Polyurethane: https://a.co/d/day228n

A suitable spar varnish: https://a.co/d/94yLy0E

Which type of Brush should you use to apply the varnish?

Make sure to choose a brush designed for the type of varnish/coating you plan to use. Finding a brush that lays down a smooth coat without heavy brushstrokes is critical for any finish. That will give it the beautiful look you're looking for.

I love Purdy and like Wooster a lot, too. From my research, these are probably the two best brushes you can buy for either a Polyurethane or a spar varnish:

Wooster Brush: https://a.co/d/4Nw8ttC

Purdy Brush: https://a.co/d/2MENOtZ

Either way, I suggest an angled brush to get into corners quickly.

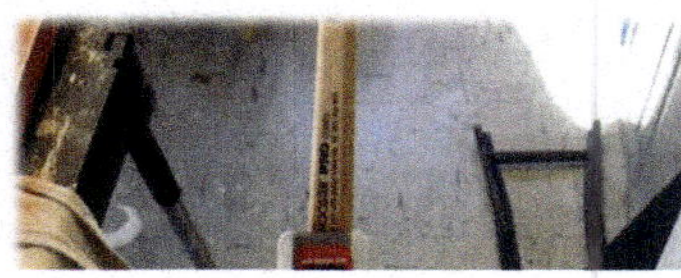

I also suggest getting one of these handy brush covers. My door took several coats, and each time I finished applying a coat, I put my brush in this cover to keep it wet. That way, I didn't have to use a new brush for each coat, which would have been expensive.

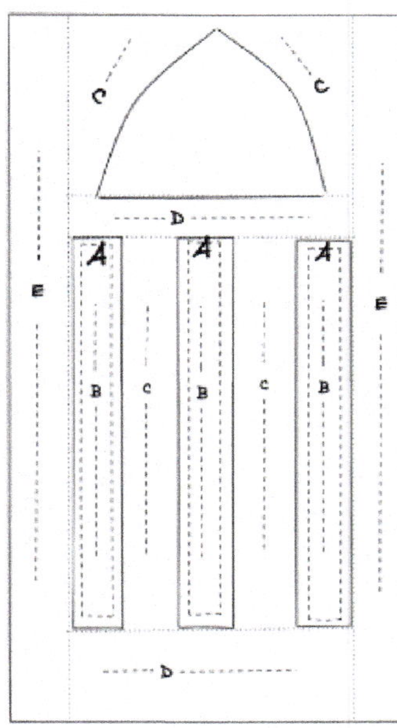

Paint Brush Cover: https://a.co/d/eNTeaY6

A little trick, though – if you can't find one of these covers, you can probably just wrap the brush in plastic saran wrap.

Process:

To varnish the door, follow the same pattern as you would if you were painting and carefully brush the finish onto the door.

Start with small amounts first and go from there. Try not to coat it too thick, and follow the grain of the wood as you brush it on. You'll see it smooth out after a few minutes as it dries.

Once your first coat has dried, it's time to give it a light sanding.

Get some 220-grit sandpaper and sand it lightly.

This light sanding aims to smooth out any bumps and other impurities to give it an even better sheen in the subsequent coating.

Once you've sanded it, use a microfiber cloth, rag, or cheesecloth to remove any sanding dust left over.

Now give it its second coating.

After it dries, check and see if you're satisfied with how it looks.

If you want to give it one more coating, follow the process again: sand it, wipe off the dust, and coat it again.

If you're happy with where it's at, move to the next step.

We are getting closer to finishing!

(More pics on the next page)

Simply use a folded sanding disk if you need to sand in delicate or hard-to-reach areas the orbital sander cannot reach.

The door after two coats of polyurethane.

STEP TWENTY-ONE
CLEAN & BED THE GLASS

TOOLS/MATERIALS NEEDED: *Glaze, Painter's multitool*

*Note: If your door has no window, skip this step and go to Step Thirty.

Clean the Glass:

While the glass is out, I recommend cleaning it with a microfiber cloth and window cleaner. You may even need a razor blade to scrape off old paint. Wherever you're scraping, wet it with glass cleaner first so you don't scratch the glass.

Create a Bed of Glaze:

To put your glass back in correctly, you'll need to get a small amount of glaze and "bed" the glass into the glaze. I recommend using Sarco - Dual Glaze. Found here: https://bit.ly/3xeUcsV

Now that you have the glaze ensure the door is flipped, so the inside/interior side of the door faces up.

Find the ledge where the glass sat and place putty into the "rabbits" (the ledge) as the picture demonstrates. Fill the rabbits up with glaze all around the window hole, as the pictures show.

Bed the Glass:

Now take the glass and carefully place it into the space.

It will press and smoosh the glaze down. Spread your fingers wide and gently press around the edges to securely bed the glass into the glaze. When you're done, it should feel thoroughly smooshed into the glaze.

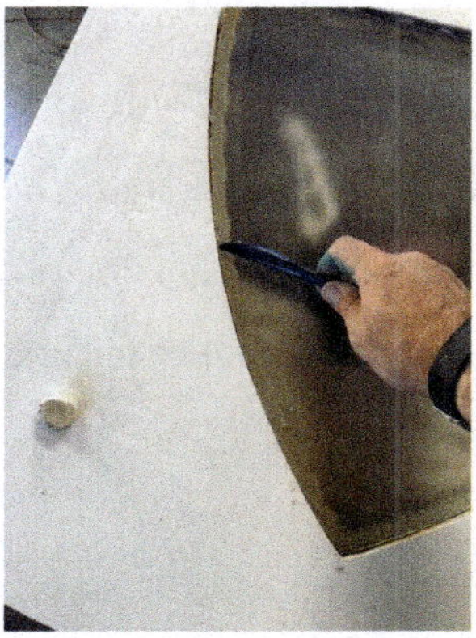

Next, use a spatula or a plastic knife to wipe away the excess glaze that smooshed through.

This picture on the right shows how I've cleaned one side of any extra glaze. You can still see the glaze on the other side. Also, you can see some excess glaze on the bottom rabbit, where I haven't cleaned yet.

Don't flip the door yet, or the glass will fall out.

STEP TWENTY-TWO

PUT WHITING ON THE GLASS

TOOLS/MATERIALS NEEDED: *Whiting, cheap unused paintbrush, Rag, Shop Vac (if available)*

<u>*Note: If your door has no window, skip this step and go to Step Thirty.</u>

<u>*Note: Use a mask during this process. This stuff gives me a headache without one.</u>

Now that you've cleaned away the excess glaze on this side put whiting or drywall dust onto the glass to clean up all the glazing oil. You'll see how it pulls the glazing oil right off the glass.

Vacuum up the excess dust or use a rag to clean it up.

You can buy whiting here: https://bit.ly/3Ryp1Rw

If you can't get whiting, you can also use drywall joint compound. Make sure it's not premixed. This stuff will also absorb the glazing oil. Make sure you wear a mask! You can buy a bag here: https://a.co/d/7RuNjHL

STEP TWENTY-THREE
FROST THE GLASS
OPTIONAL

---

*Note: If your door has no window, skip this step and go to Step Thirty.

Note: if you want to frost the inside of your glass, this is the time to do it. Now that your glass is bedded into the door, you can spray the *inside* of the glass with the frosting. You can find frosting spray on Amazon and sometimes at big box hardware stores.

Make sure to spray it until it looks wet, but no more than that, as you don't want it to run. Just spray it in a left-right fashion so that you have full coverage. Let it dry. Then add two or three more coats until it looks fully frosted.

Frosted Glass Spray: https://a.co/d/dfwX3Lo

STEP TWENTY-FOUR
REINSTALL THE MOULDING

TOOLS/MATERIALS NEEDED: *Hammer, Finish Nails*

*Note: If your door has no window, skip this step and go to Step Thirty.

Now it's time to put the molding back on. Remember, the molding is delicate! Be careful!

Also, ensure you've primed and painted your molding before reinstalling it. If you haven't done that yet, go back and paint it. If your molding is not painted because you've decided to varnish the inside of your door, go ahead and make sure your molding is stained and varnished before starting this step.

To reinstall the molding:

Use small finish nails and hammer them in, like in the pictures. Place nails about every 3-4 inches.

You can buy these types of nails here:

1 Inch: https://a.co/d/dxPOs8c

¾ inch: https://a.co/d/ioJMGz9

I used ¾ inch finishing nails, but if your trim is a little larger, you might wish for 1 inch.

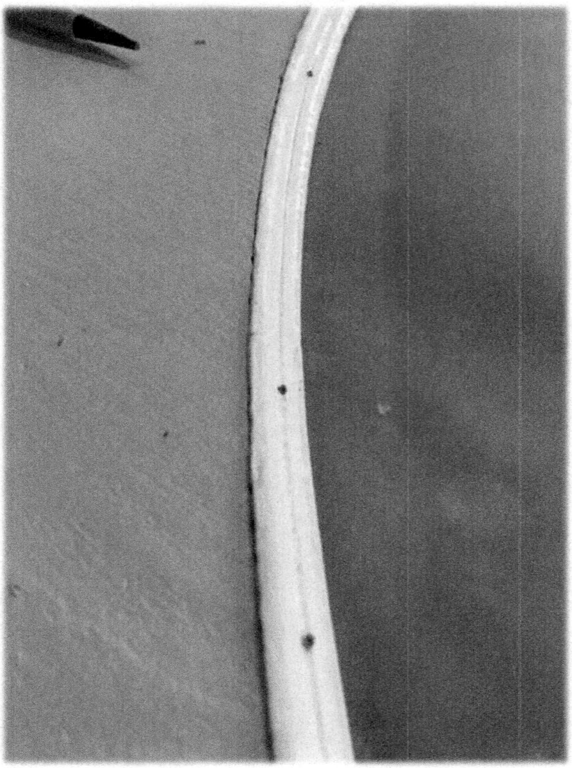

Here are the nails right before getting sunk, as described in the next step.

STEP TWENTY-FIVE
SINK THE FINISH NAILS

TOOLS/MATERIALS NEEDED: *Nail Punch, Hammer*

*Note: If your door has no window, skip this step and go to Step Thirty.

To make your job look professional, sink the nails slightly so you don't see them once you give it a quick painting.

Once the nails are sunk, fill in the little divots with some glaze and smooth it out with your finger. If you don't have left-over glaze, use wood filler or caulking.

To sink the nails, use a nail punch:

https://a.co/d/6tuSRgR

SHAVE THE MOULDING *OPTIONAL*

TOOLS/MATERIALS NEEDED: *Hand Planer or Razor Blade*

*Note: If your door has no window, skip this step and go to Step Thirty.

You can use a planer to shave any molding edges that are lifted above the rest of the door. This will help even them out and make them flush with the door, making them look perfect.

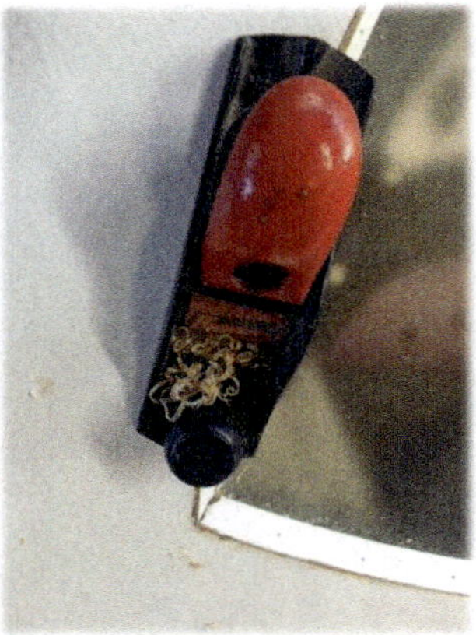

A Hand Planer: https://a.co/d/cebE8zg

To keep it cheap, you can also probably use a razor blade.

When you're done, it should look like the picture on the right. You can fill any remaining gaps with putty.

STEP TWENTY-SEVEN
PAINT OR VARNISH THE MOLDING

TOOLS/MATERIALS NEEDED: *Interior Paint or Varnish*

*Note: If your door has no window, skip this step and go to Step Thirty.

Now add a small, final coat of paint or varnish over the molding to cover the nail holes and any gaps.

If your interior side is painted, then paint the molding.

If your interior side is varnished, then varnish the molding.

Remember, less is more, and try to use minimal amounts of paint when you do this so it doesn't run onto the glass.

STEP TWENTY-EIGHT
CLEAN THE GLAZE OFF THE EXTERIOR SIDE

TOOLS/MATERIALS NEEDED: *Plastic Silverware Knife or Painter's Multitool*

<u>*Note: If your door has no window, skip this step and go to Step Thirty.</u>

Since the glass is now entirely secure, you can finally flip the door to work on the exterior!

On the exterior side, use a spatula or plastic knife to scrape away any glazing that was smooshed out from the side of the glass, just like you did on the interior side.

Create a clean, smooth line.

Sometimes a free plastic knife is the best tool of all for this.

STEP TWENTY-NINE
PUT WHITING ON THE EXTERIOR SIDE GLASS

TOOLS/MATERIALS NEEDED: *Whiting, Rag, Shop Vac (if you have one)*

<u>*Note: If your door has no window, skip this step and go to Step Thirty.</u>

Just as you did on the interior side, put whiting on the glass and swirl it around to remove any of the glazing oil from the glass.

Good job! You are all done with refinishing the door. Now you just need to put the hardware back on and mount the door. The door should look something like this by now:

STEP THIRTY
REINSTALL THE HARDWARE

TOOLS/MATERIALS NEEDED: *Small Flathead Screwdriver, Phillips Head Screwdriver*

If you took your lock to be rebuilt by a locksmith, hopefully, you have it back now, and it looks great. My locksmith polished everything up and made my lock look amazing. You can now even see the name brand of the locksmith manufacturer from 100 years ago.

Reinstall your lock and handles and put on all other hardware like door knockers. And put your hinges on.

STEP THIRTY-ONE
MOUNT THE DOOR

TOOLS/MATERIALS NEEDED: *Hammer*

<u>FINAL STEP!</u>

Remove any plywood that you used to board up the door frame.

Now mount the door.

The easiest way to mount the door is to put the frame side of the hinges back into their original place if you even removed them. Also, make sure you've installed the other part of the hinges back onto the door.

Then have someone help you slide the door into its original slot and drop the pin down into the hinges, and you're good to go. Sometimes you will need to hammer down the hinge pin slightly. Add some WD-40 if they are squeaking.

And now you're done!

Congrats!

I hope you enjoyed this process. And even if this book was as clear as mud, I hope it helped somewhat and you enjoyed the process. Thank you for reading my book! ☺

"I may not have gone where I intended to go, but I think I have ended up where I needed to be." ~ Douglas Adams

LARGER PICTURES FOR REFERENCE

Interior Door that I restored following the same process in this book.

The first day I saw my door. We were touring the house to see if we wanted to buy the house. It looked rough, but I could tell it was a unique door.

Another view of my door before its restoration.

Fortunately, my door had all the original hardware.   And the hardware was so elegant. But the door was missing chunks of wood and was in bad condition.

The lock needed a lot of work. Luckily, a great locksmith in town agreed to restore the lock.

Another view of the door. It had holes in it and was missing chunks of wood.

Some of the hardware to the door after I removed all the paint and restored it.

The original varnish stayed hidden under the door knocker for all these years. It was the only part of the door that still retained its original color. As you can see, it was once a beautiful door.

Me testing out some stain colors on some 100-year-old shiplap.

My door after I finished scraping the painted interior side of the door. It took about 25 minutes to scrape the door.

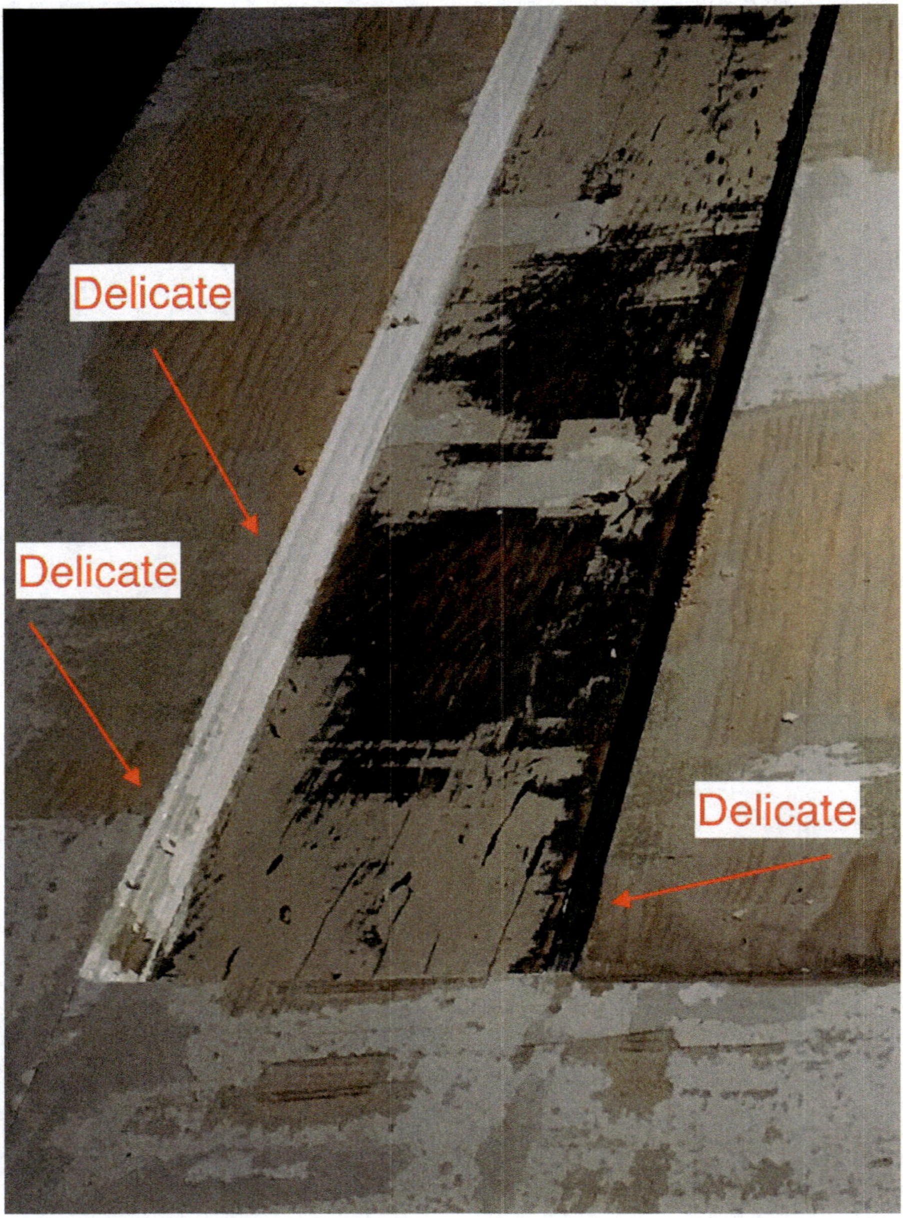

Picture of the delicate areas of the door that I would typically try to avoid scraping as I don't want to damage the door. If you need to take the paint off here, you can use chemical strippers and gently pull it off, following the instructions in this book. Make sure you neutralize with vinegar.

The painted side of the door after sanding it with 80-grit sandpaper.

The painted side of my door after its first coat of primer.

The molding that went around the glass after I had pulled it out of the door.

My door after pulling out the glass and molding.

The glass resting on an old towel after I had pulled it from the door. It needed a deep cleaning.

The interior side of the door after two coats of trim paint.

The varnished side of the door after I finished sanding off the old varnish and adding the wood filler. Notice how white the wood filler was.

Part way through the varnished side of the door's first coat of stain.

The varnished side of the door after its first coat of stain. At first, the stain did little to color the wood filler. I panicked for a minute.

The varnished side of the door after two coats of stain. Notice that the wood filler is slightly darker but still stands out.

I needed to come up with a solution.

A close-up of the wood filler after the second coat of stain. It was still off-color.

The wood filler after rubbing it with charcoal. The charcoal darkened it up and made it look more weathered.

The door after its third coat of stain and after I had applied charcoal to the wood filler. Now all the colors are blending.

After the end of the staining process, you could hardly see the wood filler.

First coat of the Polyurethane varnish going on to the door.

The door after its second coat of Polyurethane varnish. It's looking stunning at this point.

Another view of the door after its second and final coat of Polyurethane varnish.

Time to put the glass in. Here I am adding glaze to the door so that I can bed the glass into the door.

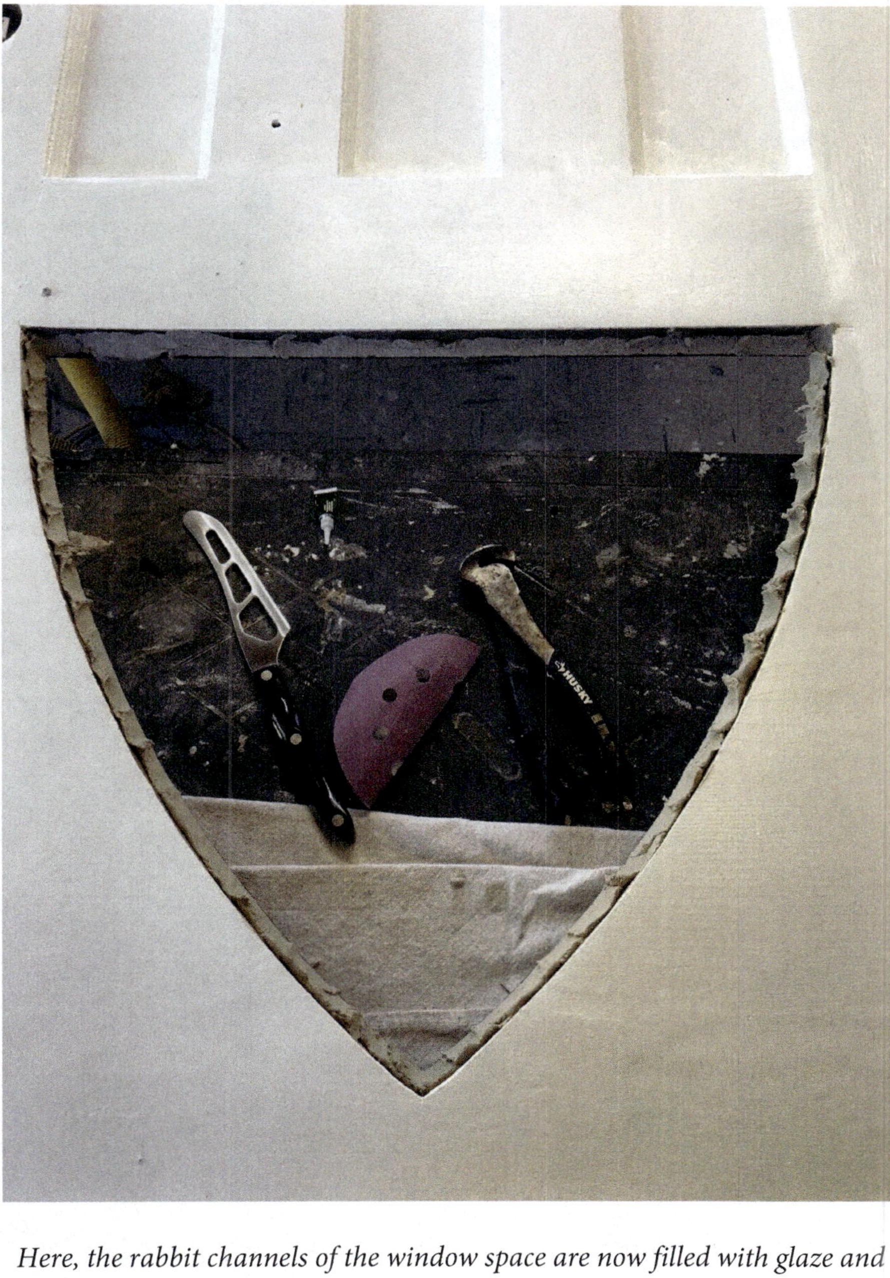

Here, the rabbit channels of the window space are now filled with glaze and ready to bed the glass.

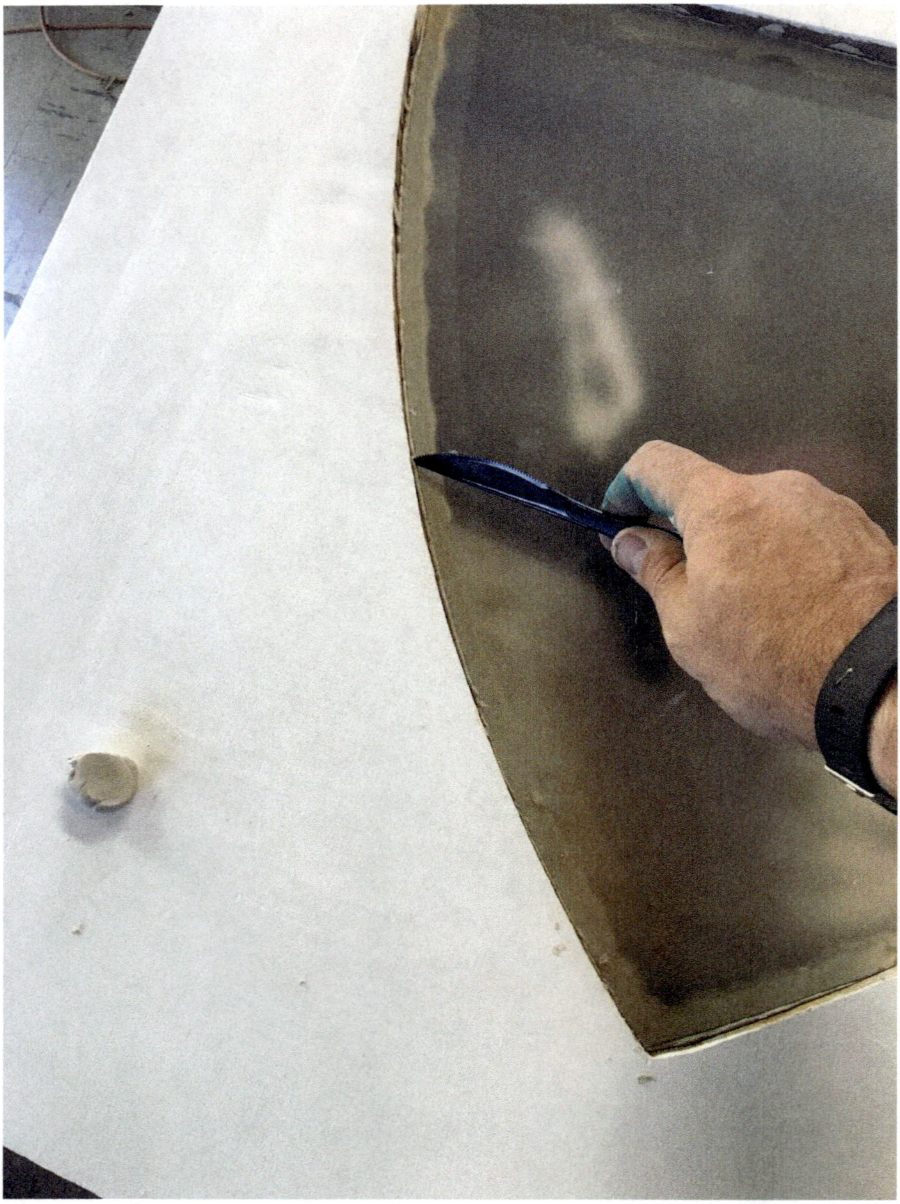

After I placed the glass in, I used a plastic fork to wipe away the extra glaze.

Whiting on the glass. Put there to help wipe away the glazing oil.

I use small finishing nails to secure the molding strips back over the glass. The glass will now be secure for the next many decades.

Here I am sinking the finishing nails so they can't be seen once painted.

Here I am putting a planer over the wood to level out the molding strips. The planer only shaved off a tiny sliver of wood, but it made a difference.

The little slivers of wood in the planer.

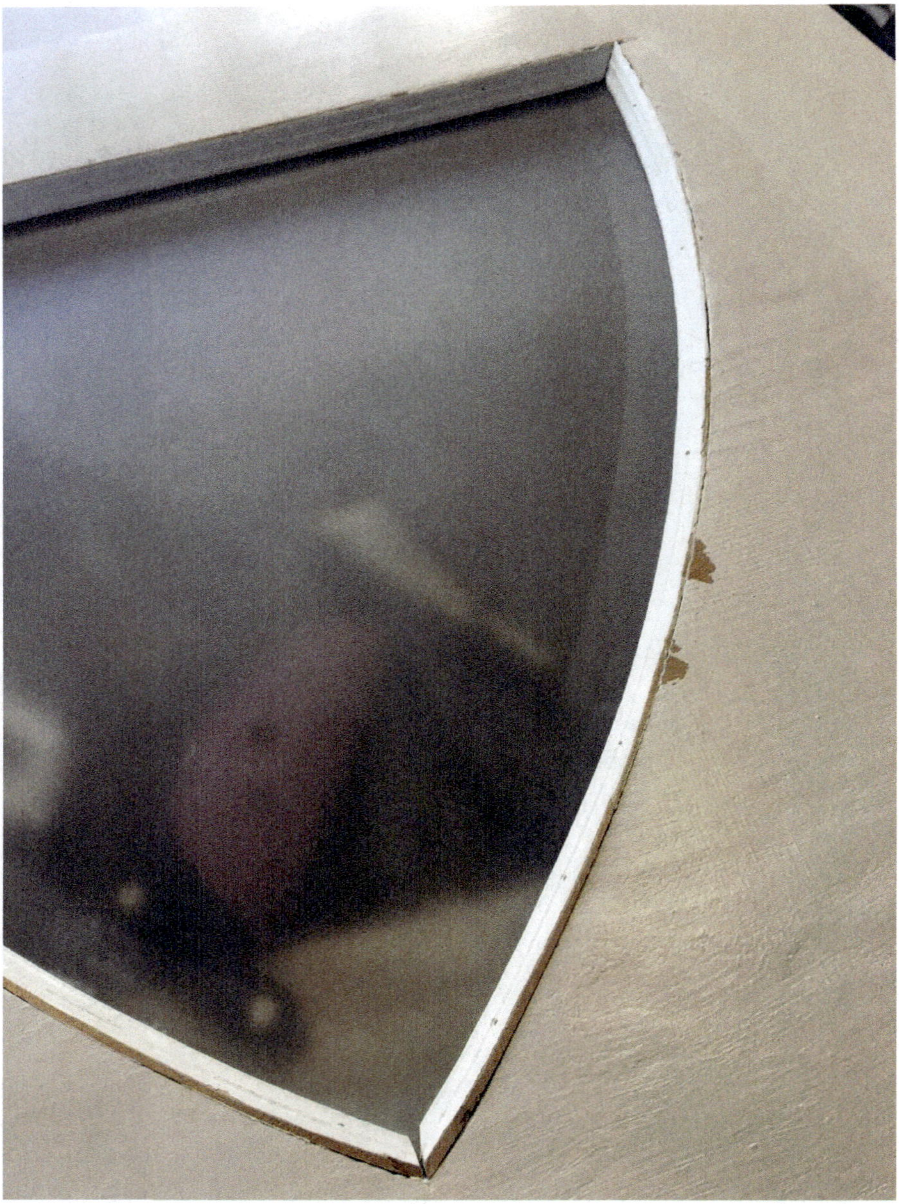

The molding after I had shaved it a bit with the planer.

There was a tiny gap between the molding and the main body of the door, so I filled it with glaze and smoothed it out.

Another view of the molding gap filled in with glaze.

After sinking the nails, shaving the molding a little, and filling in the gaps with glaze, I painted a final coat with a small brush.

Flipped the door to the other side. Here scraping away the glaze that smooshed through the front side of the door after I placed the glass in.

Another image of me smoothing away the glaze on the varnished side.

I threw some whiting on the glass to ensure no streaks were left on the glass from the glazing oil.

I am now adding the hardware back onto the door, including the hinges.

The door with both hinges going on.

My refurbished Clinton Mortise Lock. Lisa, my city's best locksmith, cleaned this lock up and made it shine. She did such a fantastic job.

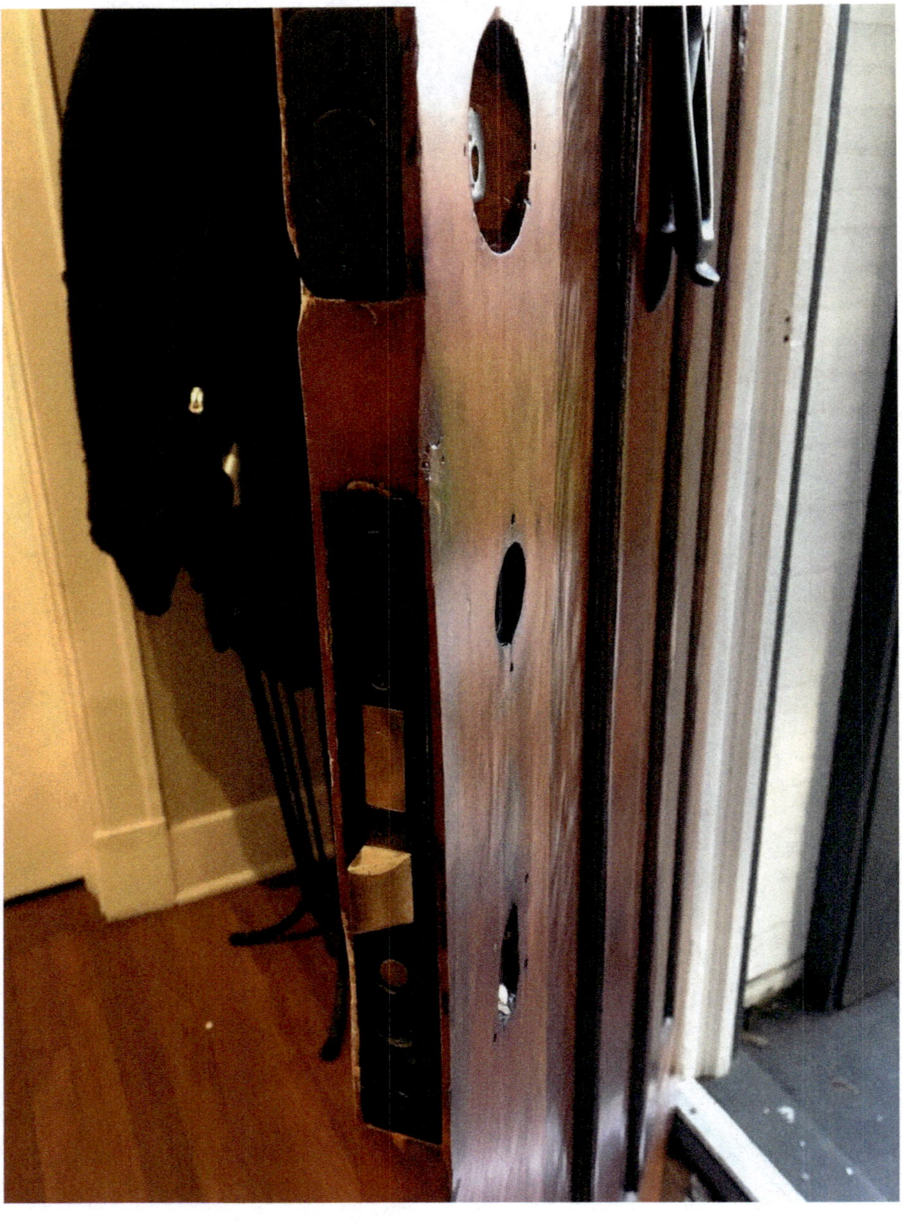

My beautiful lock is now set back into the door. The door is ready for its handles.

The newly restored door is now mounted and looking good. This was the first night after remounting the door. I loved how the light shined through the frosted glass, giving it a warm glow and welcoming vibe.

The door is now fully restored. It has new paint on the interior, new stain and varnish on the exterior, new glaze to bed the glass, and all the hardware has been cleaned up and restored. The door is now the showpiece of the house!

Thank you for your time in reading this. I hope this was a helpful guide for you!

~ Mitchell Kilby

www.lowbudgetwindowrestoration.com

THE END

ABOUT THE AUTHOR

Mitch is a technology transactions attorney who lives in San Antonio, Texas. After graduating from law school, he bought a 100-year-old fixer-upper and learned restoration techniques by talking to various folks and trial and error.

He later restored all the historical windows on his first house and then restored all the doors, hardware, etc. The techniques he learned from doing this work inspired this book.

He later created the website "Low Budget Window Restoration" to help others learn restoration techniques and to provide a resource and hub for finding restoration help, especially about historic windows.

He has restored three houses in the San Antonio area and is now slowly restoring his great-grandparents' river cabin.

His website is: www.lowbudgetwindowrestoration.com

Mitch's other publication is *The Mouse That Roared: Implications of the WTO Ruling in US-Gambling*, 44 TEX. INT'L LJ 233 (2008).